DINO DUEL

SPINOSAURUS VS. SUCHOMIMUS

Prehistoric Showdown

Tom Jackson

Lerner Publications ◆ Minneapolis

Lerner Publications Company
An imprint of Lerner Publishing Group, Inc.
241 First Avenue North
Minneapolis, MN 55401 USA

For reading levels and more information, look up this title at www.lernerbooks.com.

Main body text set in Aptifer Sans LT Pro.
Typeface provided by Linotype.

Library of Congress Cataloging-in-Publication Data

Names: Jackson, Tom, 1972–author.
Title: Spinosaurus vs. suchomimus : prehistoric showdown / Tom Jackson.
Description: Minneapolis : Lerner Publications, [2026] | Series: Dino duel | Includes bibliographical references and index. | Audience: Ages 8–11 | Audience: Grades 4–6 | Summary: "The spinosaurus might tower over the suchomimus, but this dinosaur has pointed claws and large jaws. Who would win in a fight? Readers discover a possible winner after learning about these dinosaurs' traits"—Provided by publisher.
Identifiers: LCCN 2024047168 (print) | LCCN 2024047169 (ebook) | ISBN 9798765669242 (lib. bdg.) | ISBN 9798765683910 (pbk.) | ISBN 9798765676691 (epub)
Subjects: LCSH: Spinosauridae—Juvenile literature.
Classification: LCC QE862.S3 J33 2026 (print) | LCC QE862.S3 (ebook) | DDC 567.912—dc23/eng/20250123

LC record available at https://lccn.loc.gov/2024047168
LC ebook record available at https://lccn.loc.gov/2024047169

Manufactured in the United States of America
1 – CG – 7/15/25

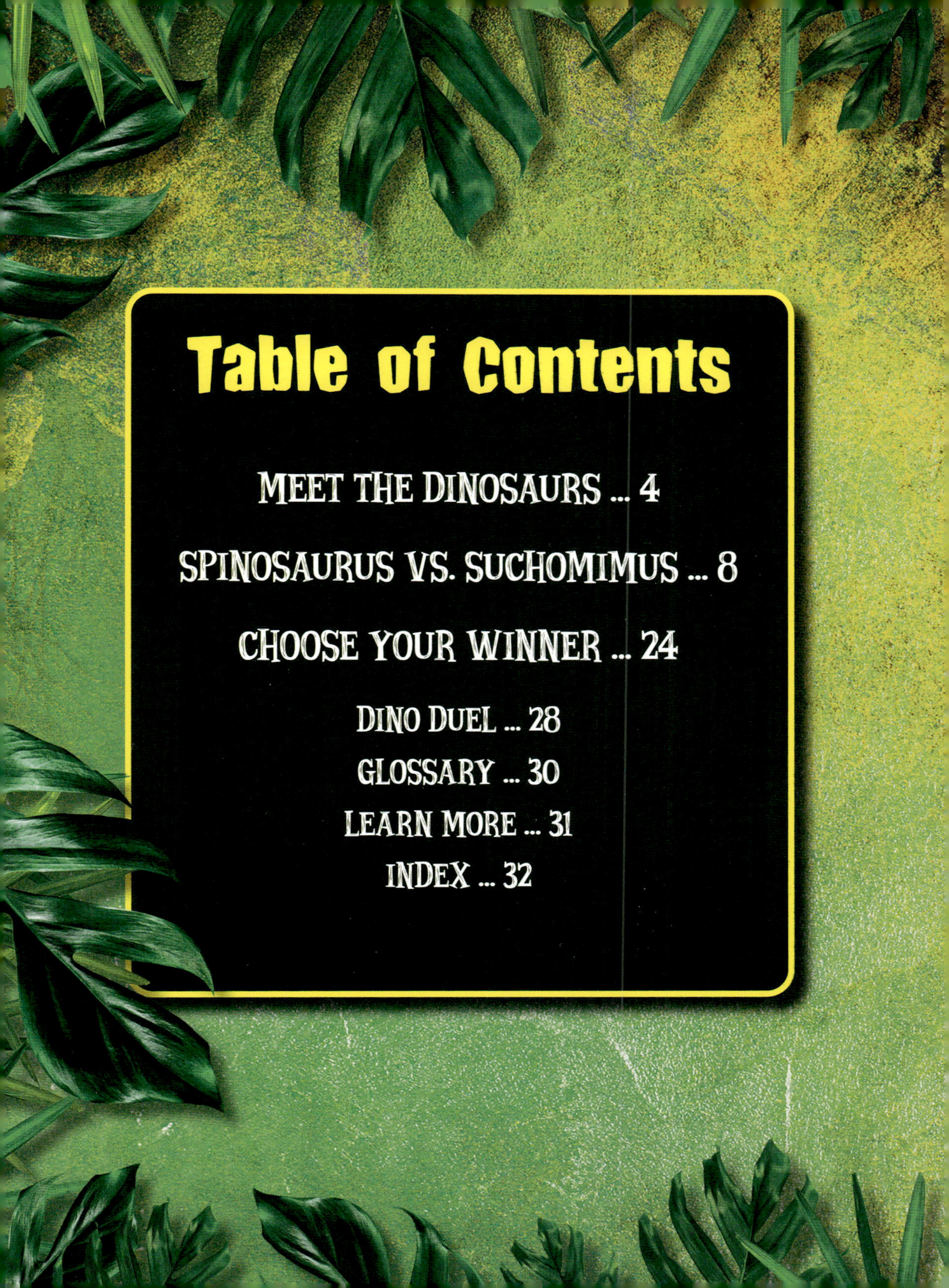

Table of Contents

MEET THE DINOSAURS

A suchomimus is standing very still. Its two feet are in the shallow water of a river. The dinosaur is looking down into the clear waters. It is waiting for a fish to swim near enough to snatch in its long jaws. Wait! There is something moving in the water. It looks bigger than a fish.

The movement is coming from the deep water farther away from the bank. All of a sudden, a spinosaurus appears out of the water. There is a sail-shaped crest on the dinosaur's back. Both the suchomimus and spinosaurus look similar. However, the spinosaurus is much longer and heavier. There is no room for both of them to hunt on this riverbank!

The suchomimus and spinosaurus lived in the same habitat.

The spinosaurus looks huge, thanks to the tall sail along its back. The suchomimus has a sail too, but it is not as big. The path to the shore is blocked for the smaller, weaker suchomimus. It cannot run away.

Both dinosaurs have long, biting jaws filled with sharp teeth. They also have long fingers on their front legs with thick, hooked claws. Using these weapons, the dinosaurs could hurt each other badly. Which one will win the fight?

DINO STATS

Spinosaurus

Weight: 7.7 tons (7 t)
Length: 49 feet (15 m)
Main weapons: Strong jaws, sharp teeth, a long, powerful tail

Suchomimus

Weight: 4.2 tons (3.8 t)
Length: 36 feet (11 m)
Main weapons: Pointed claws, long jaws with hooked teeth

SPINOSAURUS VS. SUCHOMIMUS

A spinosaurus catches and eats a shark.

Suchomimuses and spinosauruses lived in what is now North Africa around one hundred million years ago. Today this area is dry and has large areas of sandy deserts. When these two dinosaurs were alive, the area was very different. Parts of the land were covered by shallow seas and there were many rivers. This was where the two dinosaurs lived and hunted.

There were no people around back then. Everything we know about spinosauruses and suchomimuses comes from fossil bones, teeth, and footprints. Scientists use the fossils to recreate what the dinosaurs looked like. The scientists also look for other clues in the rocks nearby. These can help show what sort of place the dinosaurs lived in.

Big Beasts

Both types of dinosaurs were large. The suchomimus was as long as a school bus. However, it looked small compared to the spinosaurus. The spinosaurus was the size of a semitruck, and it weighed about the same as well. It was almost twice as heavy as a suchomimus.

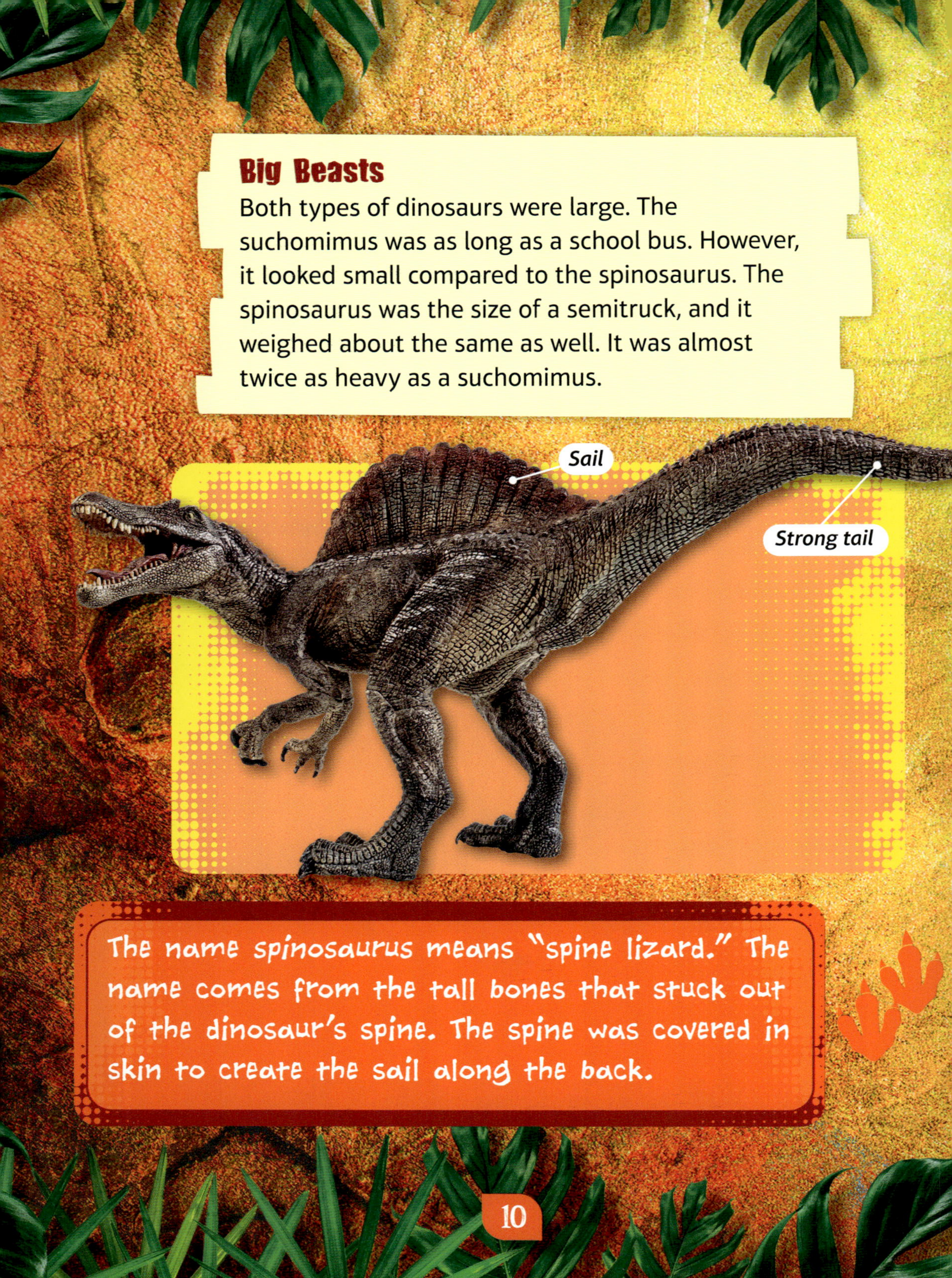

The name spinosaurus means "spine lizard." The name comes from the tall bones that stuck out of the dinosaur's spine. The spine was covered in skin to create the sail along the back.

The spinosaurus is the biggest hunting dinosaur discovered so far. It was longer and heavier than a T. rex or an allosaurus. However, these two predators were both taller than a spinosaurus. Being heavy helped spinosauruses defend themselves from other dinosaurs. Spinosauruses would also have fought each other over food and mates.

The spinosaurus hunted animals on land and in the water.

Moving at Speed

Spinosauruses and suchomimuses belong to a large group of dinosaurs called theropods. Other theropods include giganotosauruses and velociraptors. All theropods walked on their two back legs. They leaned forward so their back was flat, not upright. The dinosaurs kept their balance using their long tail. This was held out backward to balance the head and body at the front.

The suchomimus ate fish and other smaller water animals.

Spinosauruses and suchomimuses spent their time walking through water. They had shorter legs than other theropods. This shows they were not as fast at running as other predators that lived on land. A spinosaurus could run at about 15 miles (25 km) an hour. That's about as fast as a bull. A suchomimus was a little faster.

The suchomimus was more agile than the spinosaurus. It was able to scurry and leap around in shallow water to catch its prey. The spinosaurus would wait quietly for prey, then attack by surprise.

Finding Food

The shape of the jaws of a suchomimus and a spinosaurus tells scientists that they ate a lot of fish. They had a long, narrow snout that was filled with many sharp teeth. A spinosaurus's teeth were straight. A suchomimus's teeth were more hooked. Hooked teeth helped it hold onto fish and other prey. Many of today's fish eaters, such as river dolphins and crocodiles, have this same mouth.

Tooth gap

A suchomimus's snout was 4 feet (1.2 m) long and its mouth had more than one hundred teeth.

The name *suchomimus* means "like a crocodile." These dinosaurs used their jaws to grab fish. The sharp teeth grabbed hold of the slippery prey. The dinosaurs also had a gap in the teeth at the front of their mouth. This made room for the long teeth above and below as the dinosaurs bit their prey.

In the Water

Scientists do not have complete fossil skeletons for either the spinosaurus or the suchomimus. That means they are not completely sure how these dinosaurs moved in the water. A suchomimus had small bones with air inside. This dinosaur would have floated well and found it hard to dive underwater.

Spinosauruses often waded through the water.

Both dinosaurs' nostrils were on top of the snout. They could breathe even when the rest of their body was under the water.

A suchomimus spent most of its time in shallow water.

A spinosaurus's bones were much heavier than those of a suchomimus. It probably moved like a hippo does today. It could walk along the deep water of a riverbed and could swim for short distances. It probably used its tail like an oar, waving it from side to side.

Hands and Claws

The suchomimus probably spent most of its time wading in shallow water. No one is sure, but the dinosaur might have used its arms to scoop fish from the water. The three hooked claws on each hand would help with that. Grizzly bears can catch fish like this today.

A fish could not escape once it was trapped in a suchomimus's toothy mouth.

Scientists think that spinosauruses and suchomimuses hunted along the seashore. This means that they probably preyed on flying reptiles called pterosaurs that were also in this area.

The spinosaurus was among the fiercest predators in the river.

The spinosaurus was too big to move fast in water. It may also have hunted dinosaurs that came down to the river to drink. The spinosaurus would rush out of the water and grab them with its hooked claws. It would then pull them back into the water. Crocodiles hunt like this today.

Using the Sail

Both dinosaurs had a set of tall bones running down their back. These bones formed a sail-like structure. No one is quite sure what it was for. The sail created a large area of skin. This might have been used for picking up the warmth of the sunshine. That helped the dinosaurs get warm and dry more quickly.

The spinosaurus had one of the biggest sails of any type of dinosaur.

The spinosaurus might have been able to swim down into deeper water.

It is also possible that the sail helped the dinosaurs as they were swimming. It would stop them from rolling over in the water. Their legs would hang down under their body to keep the dinosaur the right way up.

Spinosauruses had a very tall sail. It is thought the sail helped them get attention from mates. The male spinosauruses may have had bigger sails to show off to the females.

A velociraptor (*right*) would stay away from a suchomimus.

Using Weapons

Both the spinosaurus and suchomimus hunted for prey that were much smaller than they were. They attacked prey using their sharp teeth and claws, and perhaps their tails. They would have used these same weapons in fights with rivals over mates.

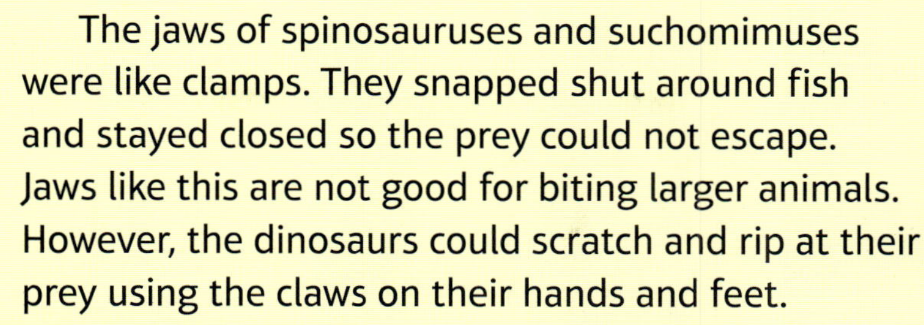

The jaws of spinosauruses and suchomimuses were like clamps. They snapped shut around fish and stayed closed so the prey could not escape. Jaws like this are not good for biting larger animals. However, the dinosaurs could scratch and rip at their prey using the claws on their hands and feet.

Spinosauruses probably fought each other when they met.

The spinosaurus might have killed whole schools of fish by slapping them with its flat tail. The slap would stun the fish, making it easy for the dinosaur to eat them.

CHOOSE YOUR WINNER

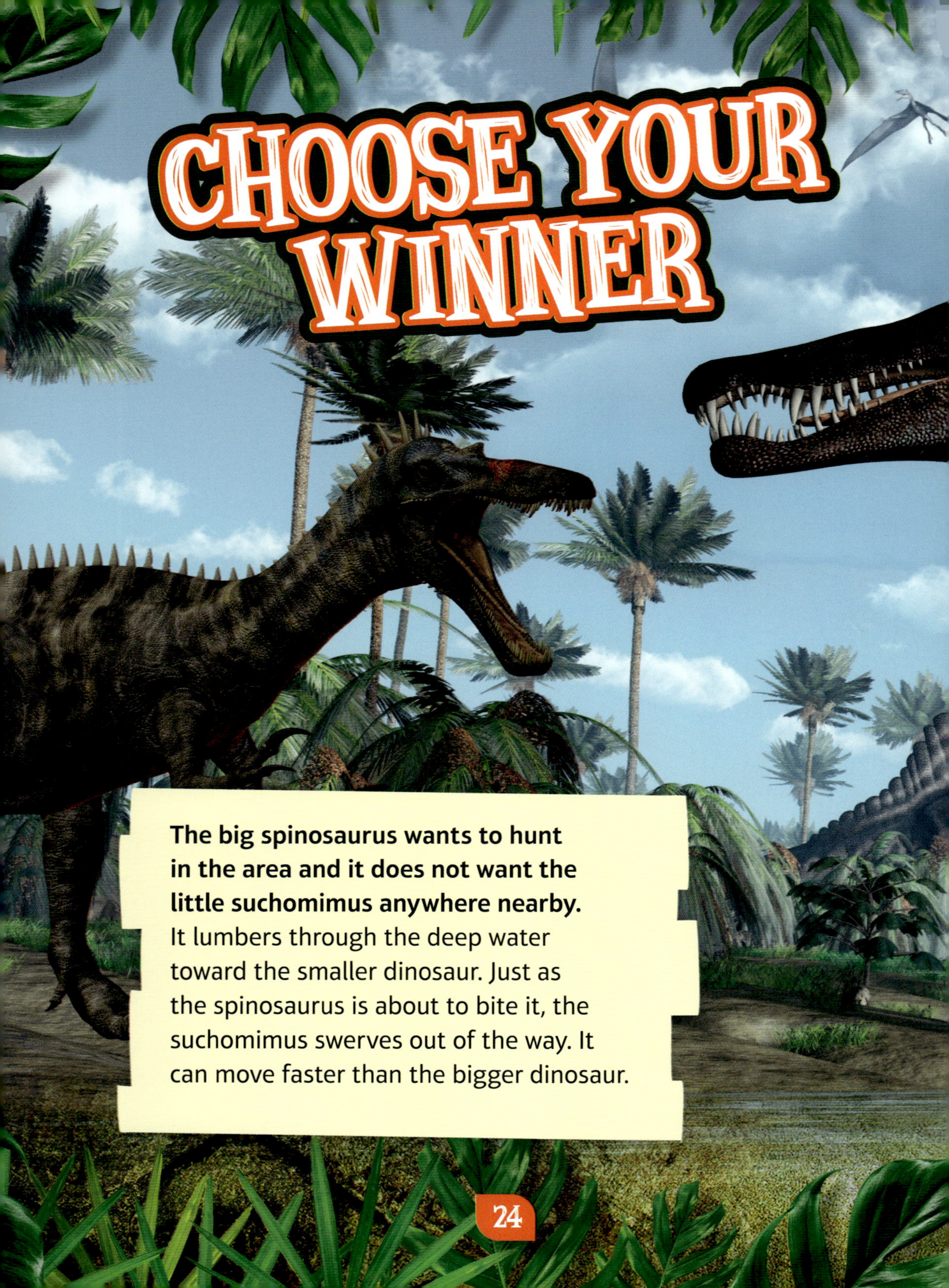

The big spinosaurus wants to hunt in the area and it does not want the little suchomimus anywhere nearby. It lumbers through the deep water toward the smaller dinosaur. Just as the spinosaurus is about to bite it, the suchomimus swerves out of the way. It can move faster than the bigger dinosaur.

The suchomimus slashes at the spinosaurus's sail as it runs past. The spinosaurus is hurt. The suchomimus is now behind the spinosaurus. To get to the shallow water and the river bank, it will need to run around the huge hunter again. It isn't fast enough this time. The spinosaurus swipes at the suchomimus with its tail. The suchomimus cannot get past.

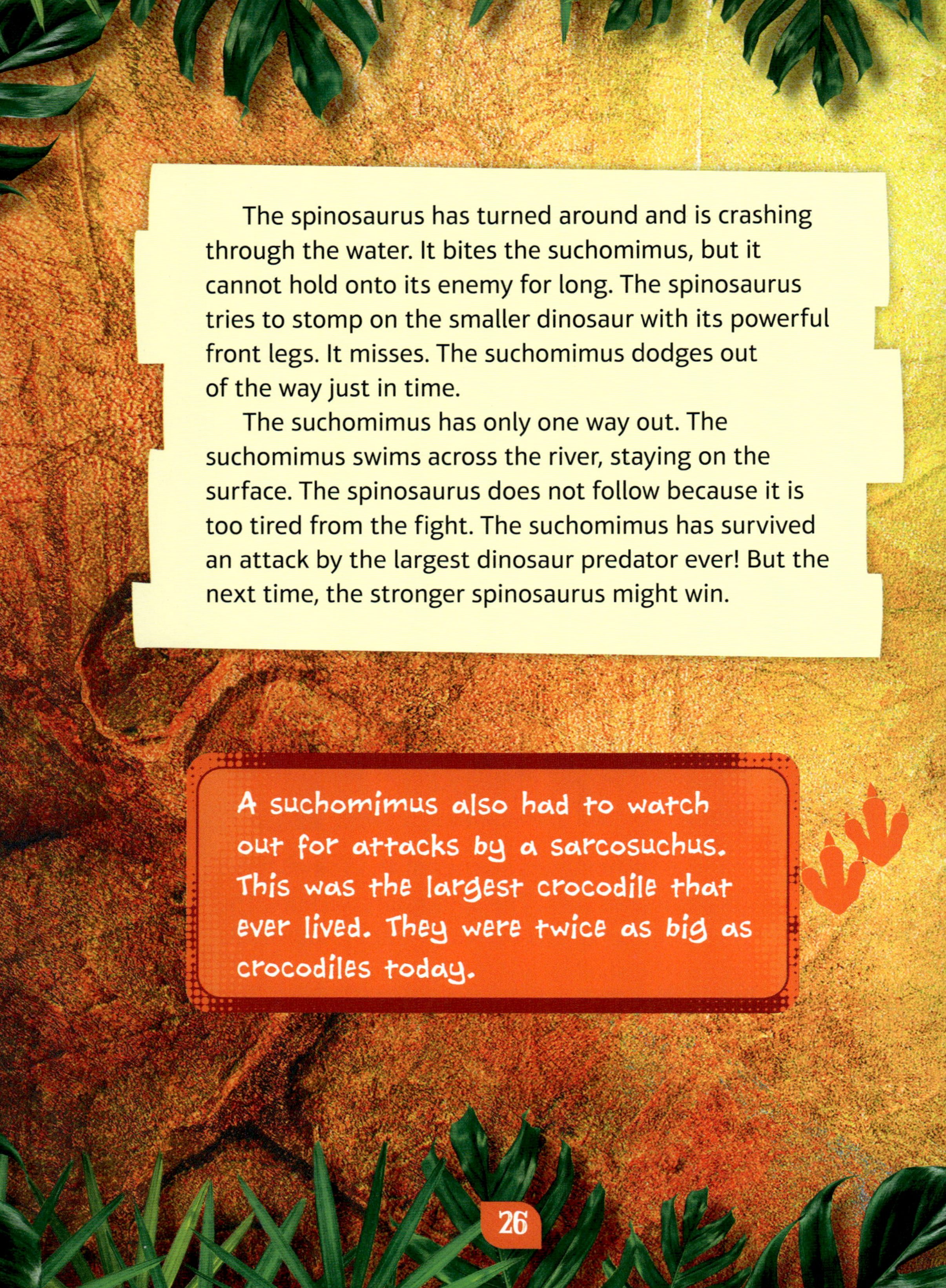

The spinosaurus has turned around and is crashing through the water. It bites the suchomimus, but it cannot hold onto its enemy for long. The spinosaurus tries to stomp on the smaller dinosaur with its powerful front legs. It misses. The suchomimus dodges out of the way just in time.

The suchomimus has only one way out. The suchomimus swims across the river, staying on the surface. The spinosaurus does not follow because it is too tired from the fight. The suchomimus has survived an attack by the largest dinosaur predator ever! But the next time, the stronger spinosaurus might win.

A suchomimus also had to watch out for attacks by a sarcosuchus. This was the largest crocodile that ever lived. They were twice as big as crocodiles today.

The
suchomimus
wins!

DINO DUEL

Spinosaurus

- Long claws
- Sharp teeth
- Tall sail along the back
- Strong jaw

Suchomimus

- Hooked teeth
- Fast running speed
- Agile
- Thick claws

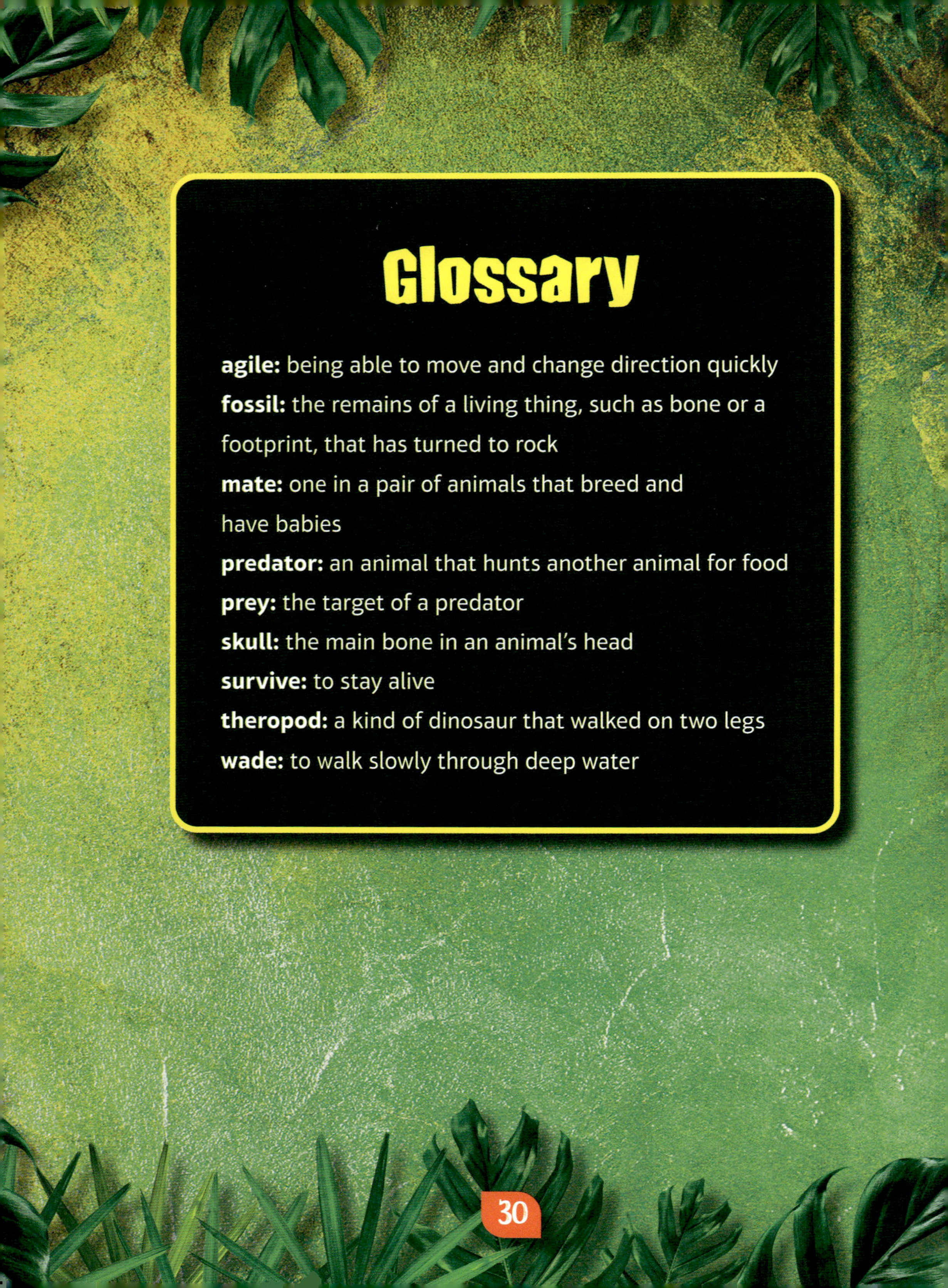

Glossary

agile: being able to move and change direction quickly

fossil: the remains of a living thing, such as bone or a footprint, that has turned to rock

mate: one in a pair of animals that breed and have babies

predator: an animal that hunts another animal for food

prey: the target of a predator

skull: the main bone in an animal's head

survive: to stay alive

theropod: a kind of dinosaur that walked on two legs

wade: to walk slowly through deep water

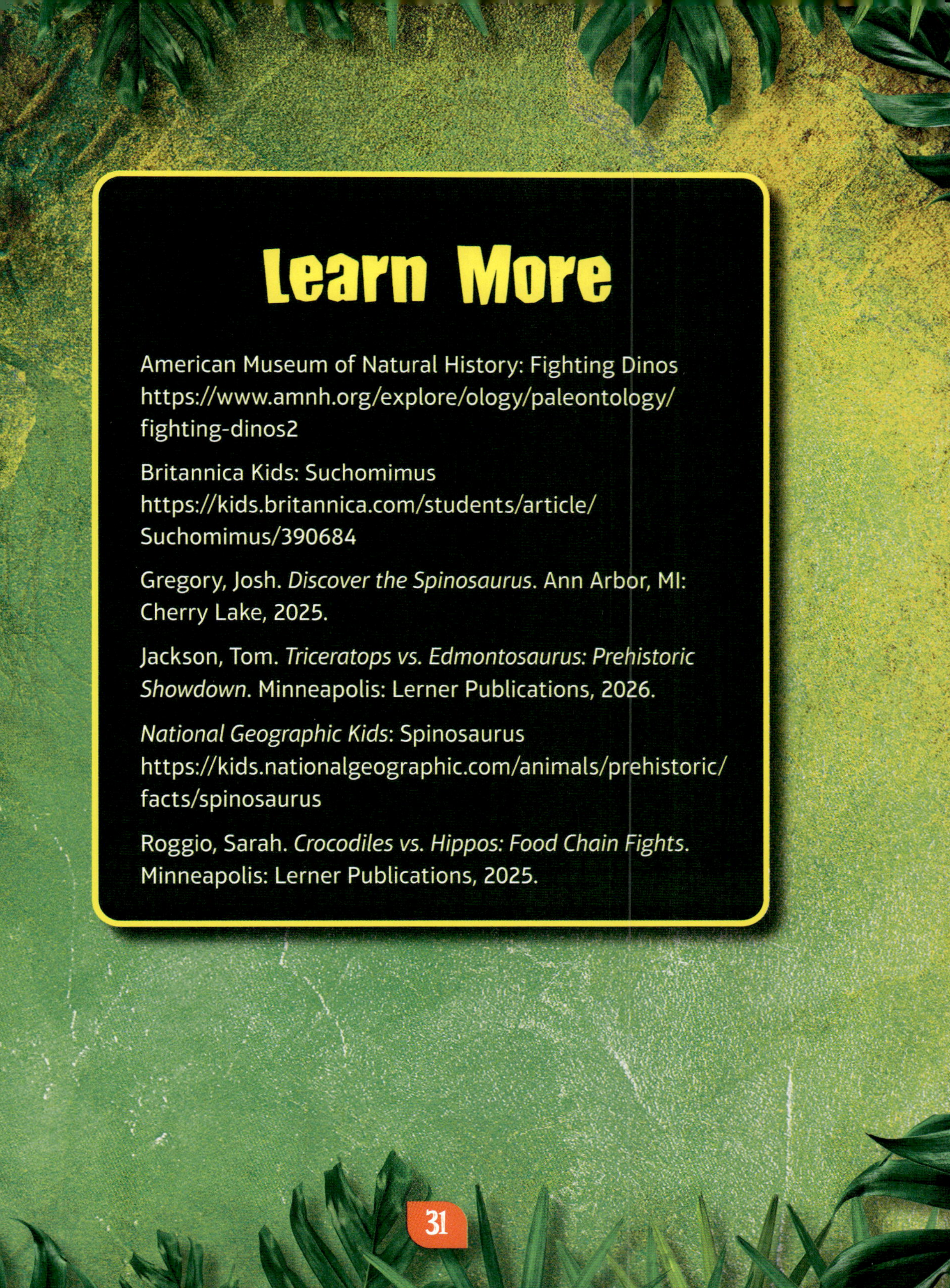

Learn More

American Museum of Natural History: Fighting Dinos
https://www.amnh.org/explore/ology/paleontology/fighting-dinos2

Britannica Kids: Suchomimus
https://kids.britannica.com/students/article/Suchomimus/390684

Gregory, Josh. *Discover the Spinosaurus*. Ann Arbor, MI: Cherry Lake, 2025.

Jackson, Tom. *Triceratops vs. Edmontosaurus: Prehistoric Showdown*. Minneapolis: Lerner Publications, 2026.

National Geographic Kids: Spinosaurus
https://kids.nationalgeographic.com/animals/prehistoric/facts/spinosaurus

Roggio, Sarah. *Crocodiles vs. Hippos: Food Chain Fights*. Minneapolis: Lerner Publications, 2025.

Index

Photo Acknowledgments

Image credits: Liidia/Shutterstock, p. 1; Vac/Dreamstime.com, p. 4; Andriy Mishchak/Dreamstime.com, p. 4; Daniel Eskridge/Dreamstime.com, pp. 5, 20; Orla/Shutterstock, pp. 6, 16, 22; Andreas Meyer Shutterstock, p. 6; kamomeen/Shutterstock, pp. 7a, 10, 29; Corey A Ford/Shutterstock, p. 7b; Herschel Hoffmeyer/Shutterstock, pp. 8, 19; Ton Ponchai/Shutterstock p. 9; YuRi Photolife/Shutterstock, p. 11; Linda Bucklin/Dreamstime.com, p. 12, 24–25; Elena Duvernay/Dreamstime.com, pp. 13, 17, 23; Warpaint/Shutterstock, p. 14; Ralf Kraft/Dreamstime.com, p. 15; Elenarts/Shutterstock, p. 18 GusTrex/Wikimedia Commons, p. 21; Mr1805/Dreamstime.com, p. 27; Nahuel Condino/Dreamstime.com, p. 28. Design elements: Kompaniets Taras/Shutterstock; Chaiyapong/Shutterstock.

Cover: Liidia/Shutterstock; Kompaniets Taras/Shutterstock; Chaiyapong/Shutterstock; YuRi Photolife/Shutterstock (top); Nikolay 007/Shutterstock (top); e71lena/Shutterstock (bottom); Catmando/Shutterstock (bottom).